This book belongs to

_____

Chicken Soup for the Soul® at Christmas

VERMILION
LONDON

1 3 5 7 9 10 8 6 4 2

Copyright © 1997 Jack Canfield and Mark Victor Hansen

The right of Jack Canfield and Mark Victor Hansen to be identified as the Authors of this work has been asserted by them in accordance with the Copyright, Designs and Patents Act, 1988.

All rights reserved. No part of this publication may be reproduced, stored in a retrieval system, or transmitted in any form or by any means, electronic, mechanical, photocopying, recording or otherwise, without the prior permission of the copyright owners.

First published by Andrews McMeel Publishing, Kansas City.
This edition published in 1999 by Vermilion,
an imprint of Ebury Press, Random House,
20 Vauxhall Bridge Road, London SW1V 2SA
www.randomhouse.co.uk

The Random House Group Limited Reg. No. 954009

Papers used by Vermilion are natural, recyclable products made from wood grown in sustainable forests

Printed in Italy by Graphicom

A CIP catalogue record for this book is available from the British Library

ISBN 0-09-182577 6

Chicken Soup for the Soul® at Christmas

Inspired by the international bestseller

Chicken Soup for the Soul®

by Jack Canfield and Mark Victor Hansen

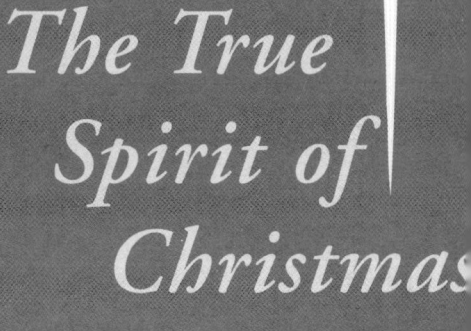

The True Spirit of Christmas

By Carolyn S. Steele

One more hour, I thought. *Just one more hour* and I'm free. It was Christmas Eve and I was stuck in beauty college. It wasn't fair. I had better things to do than wait on fussy old women with blue hair. I had worked hard and fast to get four shampoo-sets and one manicure finished before lunch. If I had no more appointments scheduled, I could leave at two o'clock. Just one more...

"Number seventy-one. Carolyn, number seventy-one."

The receptionist's voice over the intercom made my heart fall to my stomach.

"You have a phone call."

A phone call. I exhaled a sigh of relief and headed up front to take the call.

As I reached for the phone, I gave the appointment pad a cursory glance to confirm my freedom. I couldn't believe it. I had a 4:30 perm.

No one in her right mind would have her hair done on Christmas Eve. No one would be so inconsiderate.

I glared at the receptionist behind the counter. "How could you do this?"

She took a step backward and whispered, "Mrs. Weiman scheduled you." Mrs. Weiman was the senior instructor, the biddy of the ball. When she spoke, no one argued.

"Fine," I hissed and turned to the phone. It was Grant. His grandmother had invited me to Christmas Eve dinner, and could I be ready by three o'clock? I fingered the diamond snowflake necklace he had given me the night before. Swallowing the lump in my throat, I explained the situation. After an interminable silence, he said we'd make it another time and hung up. Tears stung my eyes as I slammed the phone down and barricaded myself behind my station.

The afternoon hung bleak and gray, echoing my

mood. Most of the other students had gone home. I had no other patrons until the 4:30 perm, and I spent the time at my station, stewing.

At about 4:15, Mrs. Weiman stuck her pinched face around my mirror and advised me in her soft, no-nonsense tone, "Change your attitude before she gets here," then quietly stepped away.

My mood would change all right, from angry to murderous. I grabbed a tissue and whisked away the fresh tears.

My number was called at 4:45. My tardy, inconsiderate patron had arrived. I strode brusquely up front to greet a very shriveled, frail old woman gently supported by her husband. With a tender voice, Mrs. Weiman introduced me to Mrs. Sussman and began escorting her to my station. Mr. Sussman followed us, mumbling his apologies for bringing her in so late.

I was still feeling put upon, but I tried not to show it. Mrs. Weiman cradled Mrs. Sussman closely as she lowered her into my chair. When she began raising the hydraulic chair, I feigned a smile and took over, stepping on the foot pump. Mrs. Sussman was so small, I had to raise the chair to its full height.

I placed a towel and plastic drape around her shoulders, then jumped back, aghast. Lice and mites were crawling over her scalp and shoulders. As I stood there trying not to retch, Mrs. Weiman reappeared, pulling on plastic gloves.

Mrs. Sussman's gray top knot was so matted, we couldn't pull the hairpins out. It disgusted me to think anyone could be so unkempt. Mrs. Weiman explained that we'd have to cut her hair to get the mat out, and Mrs. Sussman just looked at us with tears streaming down her cheeks. Her husband held her hands tenderly in his as he knelt beside the chair.

"Her hair was her pride all of her life," he explained. "She put it up like that on the morning

I took her to the nursing home."

Evidently her hair hadn't been combed or cleaned since that morning nearly a year before. His eyes misted over, and he shuffled to the waiting room.

Mrs. Weiman cut the matted top knot gently away, revealing a withered scalp peeling with yellow decay. She worked patiently and lovingly, and I feebly tried to help where I could. A perm would eat through her scalp like acid. It was out of the question. We bathed her scalp gently, trying to dislodge the lice without tearing her hair out. I dabbed antiseptic ointment on her festering sores and twisted her sparse hair into pincurls. The curls were held in place by gel, for we didn't dare scrape her scalp with clips. Then we gently fanned her curls dry near the warmth of the radiator.

Mrs. Sussman slipped a palsied hand into her tiny bag and drew out a tube of lipstick and a pair of white lace gloves. Mrs. Weiman dabbed the lipstick softly on her lips, then carefully threaded the shaking hands into the dainty gloves. My thoughts were drawn to my grandmother, who had recently passed away — how she always put on lipstick before walking to the mailbox on the curb. I thought of stories she told of her youth, when no proper lady would be seen in public without her gloves. Tears formed in my eyes as I silently thanked God for having taken her with dignity.

Mrs. Weiman left me to sterilize my station and returned with Mr. Sussman. When he saw his wife, their mutual tears flowed unchecked. "Oh, my dear," he whispered, "you've never looked lovelier."

Her lips trembled in a smile.

He reached into his coat pocket and presented Mrs. Weiman and me each with a small nativity set: Joseph, Mary and the baby Jesus. They were small enough to fit in the palm of my hand. I was filled with love for this man and his sweet wife. For perhaps the first time in my life, I knew the true spirit of Christmas.

We walked the Sussmans up front. There would be no fee this night. We wished them a Merry Christmas and saw them outside. It was snowing lightly, the first snowfall of the season. The flakes looked like powdered diamonds. I thought briefly of Grant and the dinner I had missed and knew that on this Christmas Eve, his grandmother would understand.

Keeping the Connection

By Patricia Chase

As a mother grieving the loss of a child, the road ahead stretches long and difficult. Not having had the opportunity to complete your child's life to adulthood breaks a mother's heart over and over again. You wonder every day what he is doing. Is he okay? You pray that he is happy.

My first Christmas without my son, Justin, was a painful struggle. I just couldn't find the strength to decorate a tree with all the beautiful ornaments Justin and my daughter, Stephanie, had made over the years. Instead, I decorated my elderly mother's tree and my family shared Christmas with her. It helped us survive the first year.

The next year, I summoned the courage to put up the Christmas tree with lights, but once again Justin and Stephanie's precious ornaments remained packed away. That's as far as I got, but it was a major step.

Justin had loved Christmas, and for the sixteen

years of his life he had always helped put up the tree. In fact, since Stephanie had been away at college, he'd taken charge of the decorating. He always assembled the nativity scene under the Christmas tree, a job he especially enjoyed. My father had made the manger out of barnboards from my grandfather's barn, and I had painted the figures in a ceramics class, so it had a very special meaning to our family.

By our third Christmas I felt stronger. I needed a connection to the Christmas times past when Justin had been alive. This time I put up the tree and lovingly decorated it with the children's ornaments. Then I went to get the box containing the nativity manger and ceramic figures, which had not been touched for three years.

As I looked inside the barnboard manger, I discovered a tiny little Christmas card. The front of the card showed a picture of a little boy carrying lots of Christmas cards to be delivered. I opened the card and read the inside verse:

> *If I could just pick up and leave*
> *I'd start this minute, I believe*
> *To be with you on Christmas Eve.*

At that moment, I knew I'd make it — not only through the holidays, but also through the long journey ahead of me without Justin. I never found out how the card got into the manger, but I viewed its presence there as a gift from my son. In my heart, I knew the tiny card with its message of wanting to be together for Christmas Eve was my much-needed connection to Justin. It would see me through that third Christmas, and ever after.

Merry Christmas, My Friend

By Christa Holder-Ocker

"I will never forget you," the old man said. A tear rolled down his leathery cheek. "I'm getting old. I can't take care of you anymore."

With his head tilted to one side, Monsieur DuPree watched his master. *"Woof, woof! Woof, woof!"* He wagged his tail back and forth, wondering, *What's he talking about?*

"I can't take care of myself anymore, let alone take care of you." The old man cleared his throat. He pulled a hankie from his pocket and blew his nose with a mighty blast.

"Soon, I'll move to an old-age home, and, I'm sorry to say, you can't come along. They don't allow dogs there, you know." Bent over from age, the old man limped over to Monsieur DuPree and stroked the dog's head.

"Don't worry, my friend. We'll find a home. We'll find a nice new home for you." As an afterthought he added, "Why, with your good looks, we'll have no trouble at all. Anyone would be proud to own such a fine dog."

Monsieur DuPree wagged his tail really hard and strutted up and down the kitchen floor. For a moment, the familiar musky scent of the old man mingling with the odor of greasy food gave the dog a feeling of well-being. But then a sense of dread took hold again. His tail hung between his legs and he stood very still.

"Come here." With great difficulty, the old man knelt down on the floor and lovingly pulled Monsieur DuPree close to him. He tied a ribbon around the dog's neck with a huge red bow, and then he attached a note to it. *What does it say?* Monsieur DuPree wondered.

"It says," the old man read aloud, "Merry Christmas! My name is Monsieur DuPree. For breakfast, I like bacon and eggs — even cornflakes will do. For dinner, I prefer mashed potatoes and some meat. That's all. I eat just two meals a day.

In return, I will be your most loyal friend."

"*Woof, woof! Woof, woof!*" Monsieur DuPree was confused, and his eyes begged, *What's going on?*

The old man blew his nose into his hankie once more. Then, hanging on to a chair, he pulled himself up from the floor. He buttoned his overcoat, reached for the dog's leash and softly said, "Come here, my friend." He opened the door against a gust of cold air and stepped outside, pulling the dog behind. Dusk was beginning to fall. Monsieur DuPree pulled back. He didn't want to go.

"Don't make this any harder for me. I promise you, you'll be much better off with someone else."

The street was deserted. Leaning into the wintry air, the old man and his dog pushed on. It began to snow.

After a very long time, they came upon an old Victorian house surrounded by tall trees, which were swaying and humming in the wind. Shivering in the cold, they appraised the house.

Glimmering lights adorned every window, and the muffled sound of a Christmas song was carried on the wind.

"This will be a nice home for you," the old man said, choking on his words. He bent down and unleashed his dog, then opened the gate slowly, so that it wouldn't creak. "Go on now. Go up the steps and scratch on the door."

Monsieur DuPree looked from the house to his master and back again to the house. He did not understand. *"Woof, woof! Woof, woof!"*

"Go on." The old man gave the dog a shove. "I have no use for you anymore," he said in a gruff voice. "Get going now!"

Monsieur DuPree was hurt. He thought his master didn't love him anymore. He didn't understand that, indeed, the old man loved him very much but could no longer care for him. Slowly, the dog straggled toward the house and up the steps. He scratched with one paw at the front door. *"Woof, woof! Woof, woof!"*

Looking back, he saw his master step behind a tree just as someone from inside turned the doorknob. A little boy appeared, framed in the doorway by the warm light coming from within. When he saw Monsieur DuPree, the little boy threw both arms into the air and shouted with delight, "Oh boy! Mom and Dad, come see what Santa brought!"

Through teary eyes, the old man watched from behind the tree as the boy's mother read the note. Then she tenderly pulled Monsieur DuPree inside. Smiling, the old man wiped his eyes with the sleeve of his cold, damp coat. Then he disappeared into the night, whispering, "Merry Christmas, my friend."

The Department Store Santa

By Sally A. Breslin

"Why are there so many different Santas?" I asked my mother, tightly clutching her hand as we walked along the icy downtown sidewalk. I was five years old.

"They're all Santa's helpers," my mother answered. "The *real* Santa is the one at Leavitt's department store. You met him last year, remember?"

I nodded, not doubting for a moment that he was genuine. The Santas everywhere else, with their scraggly cotton beards, heavily rouged cheeks and drooping, padded bellies bore little resemblance to the Santa in my favorite picture book, *The Night Before Christmas*. But the Santa at Leavitt's department store — well, he looked as if he had just stepped right off one of the pages.

"Can we go see Santa today?" I asked. "Please?"

"Next week," my mother answered, glancing at her watch. "I promise."

But five days later, instead of visiting Santa, I found myself on a cold table in a doctor's examining room.

Wide-eyed, I stared at the doctor as he spouted a lot of medical terms I didn't understand… until he said, "She'll probably lose all of her hair."

"You're mistaken," my mother responded, shaking her head. "I don't want to offend you, but I'm going to take her to a specialist for a second opinion."

And she did. Unfortunately, the diagnosis was the same. I had a form of juvenile alopecia, a disease that would make my hair fall out.

I can remember watching my mother choking back tears every time she found a clump of my blonde curls lying on the floor or scattered across my pillowcase. I also remember angrily refusing to believe her when she assured me that my hair would grow back.

Understandably, I didn't have much Christmas

spirit that year. Although I felt fine physically, the sight of myself pale and bald made me want to lock myself in my room and hide under my bed. When my father enthusiastically invited me on our annual father-daughter shopping spree to buy Christmas gifts for my mother—an event I'd always looked forward to—I told him I didn't want to go.

But Dad could be persuasive when he wanted to be. He convinced me that without my help and suggestions, he probably would end up buying my mother the most hideous Christmas gifts in the history of the world.

Solely for the sake of salvaging my mother's Christmas, I agreed to go shopping with him.

Downtown, the throngs of shoppers, cheerful Christmas music and thousands of twinkling lights made me temporarily forget my problems. I actually began to have a good time…until Dad and I decided to stop for a cup of hot cocoa.

"Hi, Lou!" one of the customers greeted my father when we walked into the coffee shop. "Say, I didn't know you had a little boy! I thought you only had a daughter."

I burst into tears.

My father quickly ushered me out of the coffee shop and led me toward Leavitt's department store. "I have just the thing to cheer you up," he said, forcing a smile. "A visit with Santa! You'd like that, wouldn't you?"

Sniffling, I nodded.

But even as I stood in line in Leavitt's toy department, where Santa sat on a regal, red velvet throne trimmed in gold, my tears wouldn't stop. When my turn finally came, I shyly lowered my head and climbed onto Santa's lap.

"And what's your name?" Santa asked kindly.

Still not looking up, I carefully pronounced my full name—first, middle and last—just to make certain he would be able to find my house on Christmas Eve.

"And what would you like Santa to bring you for Christmas?" he asked.

My tear-filled eyes met his. Slowly I removed my brown stocking cap and revealed my naked scalp. "I want my hair back," I told him. "I want it to be long and beautiful, all the way down to the floor, just like Rapunzel's."

Santa cast a questioning look at my father and waited for his nod before he answered. "It takes a long time for your hair to grow, sweetheart," Santa said. "And I'm very, very sorry, but even Santa can't speed things up. You'll have to be patient and never lose faith. Your hair will grow back in time; I promise you it will."

With all my heart, I believed his promise. And ten months later, when my hair did grow back, I was convinced it was due solely to Santa's magic.

The years passed, and when I graduated from high school, I went to work full time as a switchboard operator at Leavitt's department store. All my coworkers were friendly, but one employee in particular went out of his way to make me feel welcome. He was a retired professional boxer named "Pal" Reed, the store's handyman and jack-of-all-trades.

Pal had a knack for sensing when an employee was depressed, and he did everything he could to help. When I was learning how to work the switchboard and became so frustrated over my mistakes that I was ready to quit, Pal bought me a box of chocolates to lift my spirits. He was so easy to talk to, I felt as if I had known him for years.

During my first Christmas season at Leavitt's, I went down to the stockroom one afternoon to get some gift boxes. There, standing in a corner with his back toward me, was the store's Santa, getting ready for his annual arrival in the store's toy department.

"I'm sorry," I said, embarrassed that I had interrupted him while he was dressing. "I didn't mean to barge in on you."

Santa quickly put on his beard before he turned to face me, but no beard or long white wig could conceal his identity. He was the same Santa I had told my Christmas wish to fourteen years before.

He was Pal Reed.

He smiled knowingly at me, then softly said, "I remembered you the minute I heard your name — and I've never been more thrilled to see such a beautiful head of hair."

The Christmas Scout

By Samuel D. Bogan

In spite of the fun and laughter, 13-year-old Frank Wilson was not happy.

It was true that he had received all the presents he wanted. And he enjoyed these traditional Christmas Eve reunions of relatives — this year at Aunt Susan's — for the purpose of exchanging gifts and good wishes.

But Frank was not happy because this was his first Christmas without his brother, Steve, who, during the year, had been killed by a reckless driver. Frank missed his brother and the close companionship they had together.

Frank said good-bye to his relatives and explained to his parents that he was leaving a little early to see a friend; from there he could walk home. Since it was cold outside, Frank put on his new plaid jacket. It was his favorite gift. The other presents he placed on his new sled.

Then Frank headed out, hoping to find the

patrol leader of his Boy Scout troop. Frank always felt understood by him. Though rich in wisdom, he lived in the Flats, the section of town where most of the poor lived, and his patrol leader did odd jobs to help support his family. To Frank's disappointment, his friend was not at home.

As Frank hiked down the street toward home, he caught glimpses of trees and decorations in many of the small houses. Then, through one front window, he glimpsed a shabby room with the limp stockings hanging over an empty fireplace. A woman was seated near them weeping.

The stockings reminded him of the way he and his brother had always hung theirs side by side. The next morning, they would be bursting with presents. A sudden thought struck Frank — he had not done his "good turn" for the day.

Before the impulse passed, he knocked on the door.

"Yes?" the sad voice of the woman inquired.

"May I come in?"

"You are very welcome," she said, seeing his sled full of gifts, and assuming he was making a collection, "but I have no food or gifts for you. I have nothing for my own children."

"That's not why I am here," Frank replied. "Please choose whatever presents you'd like for your children from this sled."

"Why, God bless you!" the amazed woman answered gratefully.

She selected some candies, a game, the toy airplane and a puzzle. When she took the new Scout flashlight, Frank almost cried out. Finally, the stockings were full.

"Won't you tell me your name?" she asked, as Frank was leaving.

"Just call me the Christmas Scout," he replied.

The visit left the boy touched, and with an unexpected flicker of joy in his heart. He understood that his sorrow was not the only sorrow in the world. Before he left the Flats, he had given away the remainder of his gifts. The plaid jacket had gone to a shivering boy.

But he trudged homeward, cold and uneasy. Having given his presents away, Frank now could think of no reasonable explanation to offer his parents. He wondered how he could make them understand.

"Where are your presents, Son?" asked his father as he entered the house.

"I gave them away."

"The airplane from Aunt Susan? Your coat from Grandma? Your flashlight? We thought you were happy with your gifts."

"I was — very happy," the boy answered lamely.

"But, Frank, how could you be so impulsive?" his mother asked. "How will we explain to the relatives who spent so much time and gave so much love shopping for you?"

His father was firm. "You made your choice, Frank. We cannot afford any more presents."

His brother gone, his family disappointed in him, Frank suddenly felt dreadfully alone. He had not expected a reward for his generosity. For he knew that a good deed always should be its own reward. It would be tarnished otherwise. So he did not want his gifts back, however, he wondered if he would ever again truly recapture joy in his life.

He thought he had this evening, but it had been fleeting. Frank thought of his brother and sobbed himself to sleep.

The next morning, he came downstairs to find his parents listening to Christmas music on the radio. Then the announcer spoke:

"Merry Christmas, everybody! The nicest Christmas story we have this morning comes from the Flats. A crippled boy down there has a new sled this morning, another youngster has a fine plaid jacket, and several families report that their children were made happy last night by gifts from a teenage boy who simply referred to himself as the Christmas Scout. No one could identify him, but the children of the Flats claim that the Christmas Scout was a personal representative of old Santa Claus himself."

Frank felt his father's arms go around his shoulders, and he saw his mother smiling through her tears. "Why didn't you tell us? We didn't understand. We are so proud of you, Son."

The carols came over the air again filling the room with music.

"...Praises sing to God the King, and peace to men on Earth."

A Gift-Wrapped Memory

By Dorothy DuNard

Every holiday season since I was a teenager Dad asked, "Do you remember *that* Christmas Eve? Remember those two little children who asked us for carfare?"

Yes, I remembered. Even if my father had not reminded me of that strange event every season for more than thirty-five years, I would have remembered.

It was 1935, a typical Christmas Eve in St. Louis, Missouri. Streetcars clang-clanged their warnings. Shoppers rushed in and out of stores for last-minute gifts. Even then, mothers forgot a few ingredients absolutely necessary to complete the family Christmas dinner. Mother had sent Dad and me on such a mission.

Our frosty breaths made a parallel trail behind us as we hurried from the car to her favorite grocery store on Delmar Avenue. Mother liked Moll's because its shelves were stocked with exotic condiments and fancy foods.

Up and down the aisles we hurried, selecting anise and cardamom for Christmas breakfast bread, double whipping cream and jumbo pecans for pumpkin pies, and day-old bread for a fat gobbler's stuffing. We checked the last item off Mother's list and paid the cashier.

Once again we braced our backs for the frigid cold. As we stepped out of the store, a small voice asked, "Please, would you give us a dime for carfare so we can go home?"

Taken aback, Dad stopped. Our eyes met those of a little girl around nine years old. She was holding the gloveless hand of her six-year-old brother.

"Where do you live?" Dad asked.

"On Easton Avenue" was the reply.

We were amazed. Here it was night—Christmas Eve night—and these two children were more than three miles from home.

"What are you doing so far from home?" Dad asked her.

"We had only enough money to ride the streetcar here," she said. "We came to ask for money to buy food for Christmas. But no one gave us any and we are afraid to walk home." Then she told us that their father was blind, their mother was sick, and there were five other children at home.

My dad was a strong-willed urban businessman. But his heart was soft and warm, just like the little girl's brown eyes. "Well, the first thing I think we should do is shop for groceries," he announced, taking her hand. Her brother promptly reached for mine.

Once again we hurried up and down Moll's aisles. This time Dad selected two plump chickens, potatoes, carrots, milk, bread, oranges, apples, bananas, candy and nuts. When we left the store, we had two huge sacks of groceries to carry to the car and two small trusting children in tow

They gave us directions to Easton Avenue. "Home" was upstairs in a large, old brick building. The first floor housed commercial establishments, while rental units were on the second. A bare light bulb on a long cord hung from the ceiling at the landing, swaying slightly as we climbed the long flight of worn wooden steps to their apartment.

The little girl and her brother burst through the door announcing the arrival of two sacks of groceries. The family was just as she had described: The father was blind and the mother was ill in bed. Five other children, most of them with colds, were on the floor.

Dad introduced himself. First on one foot and then the other, concerned that he would embarrass the father, he continued, "Uh…er…Merry Christmas." He set the groceries on a table.

The father said, "Thank you. My name is Earl Withers."

"Withers?" Dad turned sharply. "You wouldn't know Hal Withers, would you?"

"Sure do. He's my uncle."

Both Dad and I were stunned. My aunt was married to Hal Withers. Although we were not blood relatives, we felt related to Uncle Hal. How could the sad plight of this family be? Why were they in such need when they had so many relatives living in the same city? A strange coincidence, indeed.

Or was it?

Through the years the incident haunted us. Each succeeding year seemed to reveal a different answer to the question, "What was the meaning of that Christmas Eve?"

At first, the phrase repeatedly quoted by elderly aunts, "God works in strange and mysterious ways," surfaced. Perhaps Dad acted out the Good Samaritan role. That was it! God had a job for us to do and fortunately we did it.

Another year passed. It was not a satisfactory answer. What was? If I am my brother's keeper, am I also my wife's sister's husband's brother's blind son's keeper? That was it! This tied the incident into a neat package.

Yet it didn't. The years rolled by, and each year Dad and I would again toss the question around. Then Dad, who was born in the Christmas season of 1881, died in the Christmas season of 1972. Every December since, though, I still hear him ask me, "Do you remember *that* Christmas Eve?"

Yes, Dad. I remember. And I believe I finally have the answer. We were the ones blessed when two children innocently gave a middle-aged father and his teenaged daughter the true meaning of Christmas: It is more blessed to give than to receive.

This gift-wrapped memory became the most beautiful Christmas I ever celebrated. I think it was your best one, too, Dad.

47

It's Really Christmas Now

By Kitsy Jones

The Sunday before Christmas last year, my husband, a police officer in Arlington, Texas, and I were just leaving for church when the phone rang. *Probably someone wanting Lee, who has already worked a lot of extra hours, to put in some more,* I thought. I looked at him and commanded, "We're going to church!"

"I'll leave in five minutes and be there in about twenty," I heard him tell the caller. I seethed, but his next words stopped me short.

"A Wish with Wings was broken into last night, and the presents are gone," he told me. "I have to go. I'll call you later." I was dumbfounded.

A Wish with Wings — Lee serves on the administrative board — is an organization in our area that grants wishes for children with devastating illnesses. Each year Wish also gives a Christmas party, where gifts are distributed. Some 170 donated gifts had been wrapped and were ready for the party, which was to be held that evening, less than nine hours away.

In a daze, I dressed our two children — Ben, just seventeen months, and five-year-old Kate — and we went to church. In between services, I told friends and the pastors about what had happened. The president of our Sunday school gave me forty dollars to buy more presents. One teacher said her class was bringing gifts to donate to another charitable organization and they would be happy to give some of them to Wish. A dent, I thought.

At 10:30 a.m., I phoned Lee at the Wish office. He was busy making other calls, so I packed up the kids and headed in his direction. I arrived at a barren scene. Shattered glass covered the front office where the thief had broken the door. The chill that pervaded the room was caused not only by the cold wind coming through the broken door but also by the dashed hopes of the several people who stood inside—including Pat Skaggs, the founder of Wish, and Adrena Martinez, the administrative assistant.

Looking out at the parking lot, I was startled to see a news crew from a local television station unloading a camera. Then I learned that Lee's first phone calls had been to the local radio and TV stations.

A few minutes later, a family who had heard a radio report arrived with gifts, already wrapped. Other people soon followed. One was a little boy who had brought things from his own room.

I left to get lunch for my kids and some drinks for the workers. When I got back, I found the volunteers eating pizzas that had been donated by a local pizza place. More strangers had arrived, offering gifts and labor. A glass-repair company had fixed the door and refused payment. We began to feel hope: Maybe we could still have the party!

Lee was fielding phone calls, sometimes with a receiver in each ear. Ben was fussing, so I headed home with him, hoping he could take a nap and I could find a baby-sitter.

Meanwhile, the city came alive. Two other police officers were going from church to church to spread the news. Lee told me later of a man who came directly from church, complete with coat and tie, and went to work on the floor, wrapping presents. A third officer, whose wife is a deejay for a local radio station, put on his uniform and stood outside the station collecting gifts while his wife made a plea on the air. The fire department agreed to be a drop-off point for gifts. Lee called and asked me to bring our van so it could be used to pick them up.

The clock was ticking. It was mid-afternoon, and 6:00 p.m. — the scheduled time of the party — was not far away. I couldn't find a sitter, and my son started running a fever of 103°, so I took him with me to the Wish building just long enough to trade cars with Lee.

Nothing I had ever witnessed could have prepared me for what I saw there — people lined up at the door, arms laden with gifts. One family in which the father had been laid off brought the presents from under their own tree. It was like a scene from *It's a Wonderful Life*.

Inside, Lee was still on the phone. Outside, volunteers were loading vans with wrapped gifts to be taken to the party site, an Elks lodge six miles away. By 5:50 p.m. — just before the first of the more than 100 children arrived — enough presents had been delivered to the lodge. Somehow, workers had matched up the donated items with the youngsters' wishes, so many received just what they wanted. Their faces shone with delight as they opened the packages. For some, it would be their last Christmas.

Those presents, however, were only a small

portion of what came in during the day. Wish had lost 170 gifts in the robbery, but more than 1,500 had been donated! Lee decided to spend the night at the office to guard the surplus, so I packed some food and a sleeping bag and drove them down to the office. There, gifts were stacked to the ceiling, filling every available inch of space except for a small pathway that had been cleared to the back office.

Lee spent a quiet night, but the phone started ringing again at 6:30 a.m. The first caller wanted to make a donation, so Lee started to give him directions. "You'd better give me the mailing address," the caller said. "I'm in Philadelphia." The story had been picked up by the national news. Soon calls were coming from all over the country.

By midday, the Wish office was again filled with workers, this time picking up the extra gifts to take to other charitable organizations so they could distribute them before Christmas, just two days away. Pat and Adrena, whose faces had been tear-stained twenty-four hours earlier, were now filled with joy.

When Lee was interviewed for the local news, he summed up everyone's feeling: "It's really Christmas now." We had all caught the spirit — and the meaning — of the season.

The Spirit of Santa Doesn't Wear a Red Suit

By Patty Hansen

I slouched down in the passenger seat of our old Pontiac 'cause it was the cool way to sit when one is in the fourth grade. My dad was driving downtown to shop and I was going along for the ride. At least that's what I had told him — actually I had an important question to ask that had been on my mind for a couple of weeks and this was the first time I had been able to maneuver myself into his presence without being overt about it.

"Dad …" I started. And stopped.

"Yup?" he said.

"Some of the kids at school have been saying something and I know it's not true." I felt my lower lip quiver from the effort of trying to hold back the tears I felt threatening the inside corner of my right eye — it was always the one that wanted to cry first.

"What is it, Punkin?" I knew he was in a good mood when he used this endearment.

"The kids say there is no Santa Claus." Gulp. One tear escaped. "They say I'm dumb to believe in Santa anymore…it's only for little kids." My left eye started with a tear on the inside track.

"But I believe what you told me. That Santa is real. He is, isn't he, Dad?"

Up to this point we had been cruising down Newell Avenue, which was in those days a two-lane road lined with oak trees. At my question, my dad glanced over at my face and body position. He pulled over to the side of the road and stopped the car. Dad turned off the engine and moved over closer to me, his still-little girl huddled in the corner.

"The kids at school are wrong, Patty. Santa Claus is real."

"I knew it!" I heaved a sigh of relief.

"But there is more I need to tell you about Santa. I think you are old enough now to understand what I am going to share with you. Are you ready?" My dad had a warm gleam in his eyes and a soft expression on his face. I knew something big was up and I was ready 'cause I trusted him so completely. He would never lie to me.

"Once upon a time there was a real man who traveled the world and gave away presents to deserving children everywhere he went. You will find him in many lands with different names, but what he had in his heart was the same in every language. In America we call him Santa Claus. He is the spirit of unconditional love and the desire to share that love by giving presents from the heart. When you get to a certain age, you come to realize that the real Santa Claus is not the guy who comes down your chimney on Christmas Eve. The real life and spirit of this magical elf lives forever in your heart, my heart, Mom's heart and in the hearts and minds of all people who believe in the joy that giving to others brings. The real spirit of Santa becomes what you can give rather than what you get. Once you understand this and it becomes a part of you, Christmas becomes even more exciting and more magical because you come to realize the magic comes from you when Santa lives in your heart. Do you understand what I am trying to tell you?"

I was gazing out the front window with all my concentration at a tree in front of us. I was afraid to look at my dad — the person who had told me all of my life that Santa was a real being. I wanted to believe like I believed last year — that Santa was a big fat elf in a red suit. I did not want to swallow the grow-up pill and see anything different.

"Patty, look at me." My dad waited. I turned my head and looked at him.

Dad had tears in his eyes, too — tears of joy. His face shone with the light of a thousand galaxies and I saw in his eyes the eyes of Santa Claus. The real Santa Claus. The one who spent time choosing special things I had wanted for all the Christmases past since the time I had come to live on this planet. The Santa who ate my carefully decorated cookies and drank the warm milk. The Santa who probably ate the carrot I left for Rudolph. The Santa who—despite his utter lack of mechanical skills—put together bicycles, wagons and other miscellaneous items during the wee hours of Christmas mornings.

I got it. I got the joy, the sharing, the love. My dad pulled me to him in a warm embrace and just held me for what seemed like the longest time. We both cried.

"Now you belong to a special group of people," Dad continued. "You will share in the joy of Christmas from now on, every day of the year, not only on a special day. For now, Santa Claus lives in your heart just like he lives in mine. It is your responsibility to fulfill the spirit of giving as your part of Santa living inside of you. This is one of the most important things that can happen to you in your whole life, because now you know that Santa Claus cannot exist without people like you and me to keep him alive. Do you think you can handle it?"

My heart swelled with pride, and I'm sure my eyes were shining with excitement. "Of course, Dad. I want him to be in my heart, just like he's in yours. I love you, Daddy. You're the best Santa there ever was in the whole world."

When it comes time in my life to explain the reality of Santa Claus to my children, I pray to the spirit of Christmas that I will be as eloquent and loving as my dad was the day I learned that the spirit of Santa Claus doesn't wear a red suit. And I hope they will be as receptive as I was that day. I trust them totally and I think they will.

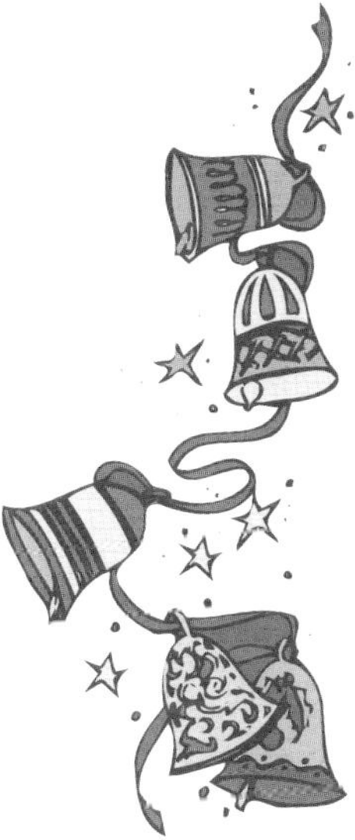

The Right Spirit

By Merilyn Gilliam

As the mother of four children, I had my hands full. Christmas was a busy, hectic time. My four children were sprawled across the living-room floor, watching television and writing down their lists of Christmas presents they wanted. My three-year-old, Ally, had the Sears catalog open and was picking out toys for Santa to bring. Joshua, the ten-year-old, was describing in great detail the different "cool" toys from the popular *Men in Black* movie. Twelve-year-old Matthew had his worn baseball mitt in his hand and was showing his father and me how he needed a new one. And Chad, our nineteen-year-old son, was writing a long list that included everything from a leather jacket to a new set of golf clubs.

On the six o'clock news on television that evening was a special feature about families who needed help at Christmas. These were families who didn't have enough money for food, let alone

Christmas presents. I noticed that all four of our children were glued to the story.

Joshua said, "Why don't we pick a family and help them out by each of us giving up one of our presents?"

"What do you mean?" I asked him, looking over sideways at my husband, to make sure he heard this, too.

"We always get so many gifts," Joshua said. "Maybe we could share some of our gifts with others."

"I think that's a wonderful idea," I said, somewhat surprised. Then, I turned to the other children and said, "What do the rest of you guys think?"

"Well, we are fortunate," Chad said. "It's hard to imagine that there are families out there who don't even have food. I think it's the least we could do, and I'm kind of ashamed we haven't thought about it before."

After a brief discussion, everyone agreed that giving to a needy family was the "right spirit" of Christmas. We telephoned the television station and told them we wanted to help out a family, preferably one with several children. We found the perfect family — one with four children ranging from a two-year-old girl to boys, nine, ten and eleven years old. The plan was for each of our children to shop and pick out a present for one of those children and give up that gift on their "wish" list.

The next night my husband and I took the children to a huge toy store. I had never seen them so excited about shopping! Ally headed directly for the play dishes, dolls and paint sets. She lovingly and carefully went through the items, searching for "just the right gift," and finally settled on a baby doll wrapped in a blanket that you could feed and cuddle.

She said, "Mommy, I know that little girl will

love this baby because it's just like the one I wanted Santa to bring me."

My heart went out to her as I watched this kind, unselfish gesture.

Joshua found the display for the *Men in Black* toys and picked out a fierce machine gun that could blast aliens. It was one that he desperately wanted to have, but he agreed to give it to the little boy of the needy family, instead.

"I'll get plenty of gifts," he said, "and that little boy will love this!"

Our nineteen-year-old picked out some toy trucks and cars that he had loved when he was a boy — a red fire engine and an ambulance. He tested them in the store to make sure they made real siren sounds. What good was an ambulance or fire engine if it didn't have sirens? And Matthew found the perfect baseball mitt.

"All children need a baseball mitt!" he exclaimed. He couldn't imagine growing up and not playing baseball.

They all proudly marched up to the cash register with their gifts in their hands. I had never seen such joy in their faces as they put everything on the counter.

My husband and I watched our children that night with pride and love. When did they get to be so wise and giving of themselves? We weren't sure how, but we were raising four children who had discovered the "right spirit" at Christmas.

Our Christmas Boy

By Shirley Barksdale

As an only child, Christmas was a quiet affair when I was growing up. I vowed that some day I'd marry and have six children, and at Christmas my house would vibrate with energy and love.

I found the man who shared my dream, but we had not reckoned on the possibility of infertility. Undaunted, we applied for adoption and, within a year, he arrived.

We called him our Christmas Boy because he came to us during that season of joy, when he was just six days old. Then nature surprised us again. In rapid succession, we added two biological children to the family — not as many as we had hoped for, but compared with my quiet childhood, three made an entirely satisfactory crowd.

As our Christmas Boy grew, he made it clear that only he had the expertise to select and decorate the Christmas tree each year. He rushed the season, starting his gift list before we'd even finished the Thanksgiving turkey. He pressed us into singing carols, our frog-like voices contrasting with his musical gift of perfect pitch. Each holiday he stirred us up, leading us through a round of merry chaos.

Our friends were right about adopted children not being the same. Through his own unique heredity, our Christmas Boy brought color into our lives with his irrepressible good cheer, his bossy wit. He made us look and behave better than we were.

Then, on his twenty-sixth Christmas, he left us as unexpectedly as he had come. He was killed in a car accident on an icy Denver street, on his way home to his young wife and infant daughter. But first he had stopped by the family home to decorate our tree, a ritual he had never abandoned.

Grief-stricken, his father and I sold our home, where memories clung to every room. We moved to California, leaving behind our friends and church.

In the seventeen years that followed his death, his widow remarried; his daughter graduated from high school. His father and I grew old enough to retire, and in December 1986, we decided to return to Denver.

We slid into the city on the tail of a blizzard, through streets ablaze with lights. Looking away from the glow, I fixed my gaze on the distant Rockies, where our adopted son had loved to go in search of the perfect tree. Now in the foothills there was his grave — a grave I could not bear to visit.

We settled into a small, boxy house, so different from the family home where we had orchestrated our lives. It was quiet, like the house of my childhood. Our other son had married and begun his own Christmas traditions in another state. Our daughter, an artist, seemed fulfilled by her career.

While I stood staring toward the snowcapped mountains one day, I heard a car pull up, then the impatient peal of the doorbell. There stood our granddaughter, and in her gray-green eyes and impudent grin, I saw the reflection of our Christmas Boy.

Behind her, lugging a large pine tree, came her mother, stepfather and ten-year-old half-brother. They swept past us in a flurry of laughter; they uncorked wine and toasted our homecoming. They decorated the tree and piled gaily wrapped packages under the boughs.

"You'll recognize the ornaments," said my former daughter-in-law. "They were his. I saved them for you."

When I murmured, in remembered pain, that we hadn't had a tree for seventeen years, our cheeky granddaughter said, "Then it's time to shape up."

They left in a whirl, shoving one another out the door, but not before asking us to join them the next morning for church and for dinner at their home.

"Oh," I began, "we just can't."

"You sure as heck can," ordered our granddaughter, as bossy as her father had been. "I'm singing the solo, and I want to see you there."

We had long ago given up the poignant Christmas services, but now, under pressure, we sat rigid in the front pew, fighting back tears.

Then it was solo time. Our granddaughter's magnificent soprano voice soared, dear and true, in perfect pitch. She sang "O Holy Night," which brought back bittersweet memories. In a rare emotional response, the congregation applauded in delight. How her father would have relished that moment.

We had been alerted that there would be a "whole mess of people" for dinner — but thirty-five! Assorted relatives filled every corner of the house; small children, noisy and exuberant, seemed to bounce off the walls. I could not sort out who belonged to whom, but it didn't matter. They all belonged to one another. They took us in, enfolded us in joyous camaraderie. We sang carols in loud, off-key voices, saved only by that amazing soprano.

Sometime after dinner, before the winter sunset, it occurred to me that a true family is not always one's own flesh and blood. It is a climate of the heart. Had it not been for our adopted son, we would not now be surrounded by caring strangers who would help us hear the music again.

Later, our granddaughter asked us to come along with her. "I'll drive," she said. "There's a place I like to go." She jumped behind the wheel of the car and, with the confidence of a newly licensed driver, zoomed off toward the foothills.

Alongside the headstone rested a small, heart-shaped rock, slightly cracked, painted by our artist daughter. On its weathered surface she had written, "To my brother, with love." Across the crest of the grave lay a holly-bright Christmas wreath. Our number-two son, we learned, sent one every year.

As we stood by the headstone in the chilly but somehow comforting silence, we were not prepared for our unpredictable granddaughter's next move. Once more that day her voice, so like her father's, lifted in song, and the mountainside echoed the chorus of "Joy to the World," on and on into infinity.

When the last pure note had faded, I felt, for the first time since our son's death, a sense of peace, of the positive continuity of life, of renewed faith and hope. The real meaning of Christmas had been restored to us. Hallelujah!

79

The True Spirit of Christmas. Reprinted by permission of Carolyn S. Steele. ©1998 Carolyn S. Steele. (*A Second Chicken Soup for the Woman's Soul*)

Keeping the Connection. Reprinted by permission of Patricia Chase. ©1997 Patricia Chase. (*A 5th Portion of Chicken Soup for the Soul*)

Merry Christmas, My Friend. Reprinted by permission of Christa Holder-Ocker. ©1998 Christa Holder-Ocker. (*Chicken Soup for the Kid's Soul*)

The Department Store Santa. Reprinted by permission of Sally A. Breslin. ©1998 Sally A. Breslin. (*A Second Chicken Soup for the Woman's Soul*)

The Christmas Scout. Reprinted by permission of Stephen C. Bogan. ©1997 Samuel D. Bogan. (*Chicken Soup for the Christian Soul*)

A Gift-Wrapped Memory. Reprinted by permission of Dorothy DuNard. ©1979 Dorothy DuNard. First appeared in *Unity* magazine. (*A 5th Portion of Chicken Soup for the Soul*)

It's Really Christmas Now. Reprinted by permission of Kitsy Jones. ©1998 Kitsy Jones. (*A Second Chicken Soup for the Woman's Soul*)

The Spirit of Santa Doesn't Wear a Red Suit. Reprinted by permission of Patty Hansen. ©1994 Patty Hansen. (*A Second Helping of Chicken Soup for the Soul*)

The Right Spirit. Reprinted by permission of Merilyn Gilliam. ©1998 Merilyn Gilliam. (*Chicken Soup for the Country Soul*)

Our Christmas Boy. Reprinted by permission of Shirley Barksdale. ©1998 Shirley Barksdale. (*A Second Chicken Soup for the Woman's Soul*)